7-18-80

GARY PLAYER'S GOLF BOOK FOR YOUNG PEOPLE

BY GARY PLAYER

with George Sullivan

A
GOLF
DIGEST
BOOK

PHOTO CREDITS

All photos by George Sullivan and
Ed Vebell except page 64, Lester
Nehamkin and pages 82–88,
Wagner International Studios.

Published by Golf Digest/Tennis
Inc., A New York Times
Company, 495 Westport Avenue,
Norwalk, Connecticut 06856

Trade book distribution by Simon
and Schuster
A Division of Gulf & Western
Corporation, New York, New
York 10020

First Printing
ISBN: 0-914178-35-0
Library of Congress: 79-55882
Manufactured in the United
States of America

Table of Contents

2104724

GARY PLAYER'S GOLF BOOK FOR YOUNG PEOPLE

From One Parent to Another

I have a special interest in golf for young people, because my wife Vivienne and I are the parents of six children—four girls and two boys. At the time this is being written, they range in age from 6 to 20. Our son Wayne, who's 18, has already begun to distinguish himself as a golfer.

I never pressured any of our children to play golf. When Wayne was growing up, he took part in various team sports at school, including cricket, rugby, soccer and swimming. He hardly ever swung a golf club.

Then in 1974 he came with me to Augusta for the Masters. Watching that great tournament inspired him. Upon returning from the trip, Wayne became really interested in golf. I bought him his first set of clubs and he began playing regularly.

By the time he was 17, Wayne had the lowest official stroke average in South Africa and had won five tournaments there. In 1978, he was chosen to be a member of our national golf team, the youngest player ever to be selected. It was a very proud moment for him and for me when he put on his team blazer for the first time. In 1979, qualifying for the British Open and the U.S. Amateur were two of his most exciting achievements.

I don't believe any parent's role can be much different from what mine has been in Wayne's case: to provide encouragement, to remain interested and to help when help is asked for.

Parents frequently ask me at what age a youngster can

Gary Player and son Wayne. A parent's main role in
helping a young golfer develop is to provide encouragement, remain interested and give help when help
is asked for.

begin golf. The answer really depends on the child's size, coordination, maturity and desire. Generally, a youngster can begin to enjoy golf between the ages of 9 and 13. But there have been many golfers who started at age 7 or 8 or even younger.

If a child begins to get frustrated by golf, it's frequently the parent's fault. A parent who wants a child to hit only good shots, and goes so far as to point out the child's shortcomings when they occur, can only retard the child's development. A parent who goads a child toward achieving some standard of perfection established by the parent can quickly destroy a child's interest in the game.

Let the child develop at his or her own pace and attain his or her own level of achievement. If the child looks forward to the weekends for the opportunity to play a round of golf, or asks to go to the driving range in the evening to hit a bucket of balls, that's fine. But if the child would rather ride a bicycle or attend a school football game, that's fine too. Accept it.

Instruction

Young people are easier to teach than adults. They're enthusiastic and eager. They're not concerned about causes or reasons. If an adult takes a swing and fails to hit the ball, he immediately asks, "Why did I miss it?" A young person in the same situation just shrugs, gets set again and says, "Watch me hit it *this* time!"

But along with being eager, young people can also be self-conscious. For this reason, they usually get more benefit from group instruction classes or clinics than one-on-one lessons. They enjoy being with their peers.

Individual instruction is worthwhile once the child is past the novice stage. Look for a teacher in your area who is esteemed for his or her work with junior golfers.

The instruction the child receives should not only sharpen skills, but also provide the golfer with an understanding of the swing so he or she can independently work on improvement.

Clinics are a fun way to learn the special techniques needed to play golf well.

Young people respond quickly to visual materials, so consider it a plus if the instructor you're considering offers such aids. Videotape equipment and swing-sequence cameras are especially helpful.

Many golf schools and camps offer top-flight junior instruction over the summer months. News of their programs and schedules can be found in *Golf Digest* and other magazines.

The United States Golf Association (USGA, Golf House, Far Hills, N.J. 07931) and the National Golf Foundation (200 Castlewood Dr., North Palm Beach, Fla. 33408) are good sources for a wide variety of instructional materials, ranging from single-page information bulletins to color films. Write to each organization for a list of available educational materials.

Equipment

There are two economical ways to outfit a young person with a set of clubs. One is to have a set of used lightweight adult clubs cut down and re-gripped. The other is to buy a new or secondhand set of clubs made especially for younger players. Clubs in a junior set are lighter in weight and have shorter shafts than adult clubs. A junior set usually includes a driver and a 3-wood, several irons and a putter.

Either way, I recommend that the fitting be done by a qualified person such as a club professional. A poor selection of equipment could hamper your child's enjoyment of and progress in the game.

Three of the most important technical considerations in fitting youngsters are grip size, shaft flexibility and club lie.

To check the size of a grip, have the golfer hold the handle in a standard grip, exerting only enough pressure to lift the clubhead from the ground. Then check the left hand. The tips of the index and ring fingers should just touch the palm below the left thumb. If they don't touch, the handle is too big.

Shaft flex is especially important in golfers who are relatively small or weak. More flexible shafts will help the young players generate clubhead speed during the swing without undue effort. Shafts with "regular" or "stiff" flex will be too hard for many young players to handle.

Club lie refers to the angle that the shaft of the club forms with the ground when the club is properly soled. If the lie is too upright, the toe of the club will be too much up in the air at address. If the lie is too flat, the heel of the club will be off the ground. Either way it will cause swing problems.

Shoes with metal spikes on the heels and soles are an important investment once you are sure the young golfer is committed to the game. They provide a solid foundation from which to launch the swing. Without golf shoes, there's always the chance of slipping when swinging.

Quality shoes that fit properly won't require a breaking-in period or cause blisters. They should fit snugly, but not tightly, at the heels. There should be about half an inch of space between toes and shoes.

Other equipment that most golfers always have with them when they play include a golf glove, a hat or cap for sunny and hot days, and a light windbreaker or waterproof jacket.

Lessons from an experienced golf professional often result in rapid progress in the game. This teacher quickly settles his pupil into a good position for swinging the club.

1. Getting Started in Golf

Next to my family, golf has been the most important thing in my life for almost 30 years, and I have never stopped enjoying it. The game has allowed me to travel from my home in South Africa and make friends in every part of the world.

Golf has been good to me financially. But while golf is my profession, it is much more to me than a way to earn a living. I also play for fun. I play golf for the pure joy I get from the challenge of the game and the challenge of a course—long fairways, lurking hazards, deep rough and fast greens. I play it for the pleasure I get from being with good friends.

I believe golf can provide more hours of fun than any other single sport. You can play by yourself or with friends, and never find it dull.

I don't know of any other game or sport that helps a person achieve independence so quickly. You stand on your own two feet in golf. Is it a 7-iron shot to the green? Or should you use an 8-iron? Should you keep the ball low and let it run? Or should you hit it high and make it bite? You make the choices. And if things go wrong, you take the steps necessary to put them right again.

You can become as good a golfer as you want to be. It depends on how much time and energy you want to devote to the game. But no matter how skilled you become, you will never completely master the game. I never have, even though I have won over a hundred championships. The fact that you never fully master golf, but always are trying to, is another of the game's great attractions.

"Beating balls" is the term the pros use for working on their games on the practice range—something every aspiring golfer has to do.

**Practice of the short game—those shots used on and
around the green—quickly leads to lower scores.**

It takes time to develop as a golfer. You can learn the
basics of many sports in a couple of hours and play fairly well.
Golf takes longer to learn because the challenges are
greater. So patience is a must in anyone who takes up the
game. Remember that players such as Jack Nicklaus, Tom
Watson and Nancy Lopez all as young people went through
stages when they were always topping the ball or hooking
into the trees or having other troubles. Scores should not be
important to you in the learning stages, either. In his first
rounds, my son Wayne often turned in scores of about 150—
more than double the par for the course. But it didn't bother
him.

Your attitude can make a big difference in how quickly

you improve in golf and how much fun you get from the game. Wayne and I were playing a practice round with two friends at a golf course in Memphis. On one hole, Wayne pulled his tee shot well to the left into some rough. "That's too bad," said one of our companions. "You're probably in trouble there. Unless the ball bounced out, you've got a bad lie."

"I'm too lucky a golfer for that," Wayne grinned. "I never have a bad lie."

Wayne really doesn't think of himself as being a lucky player. But he is a *positive* player. He shrugs off the fact that he mis-hit a drive. He walks up to the ball certain that his next shot is going to be a beauty.

You, too, will find that a positive attitude will help you play better and more enjoyably. Never take a shot without seeing in your mind's eye exactly what you want the ball to do. If it's a tee shot, picture the exact spot the ball will land on the fairway. If it's a putt, form a mental image of the ball rolling into the hole.

If you think in a negative way, by imagining your shot going into the rough or your putt sliding past the cup, chances are such things will happen.

Practice is the only sure way to learn to play golf well. But don't just practice with your golf clubs. Practice in your mind, too. Build a confident attitude and a positive outlook. These qualities will help you as much as the ability to hit long drives and sink 10-foot putts.

In talking about the swing throughout this book, I have described many drills and exercises for improving specific golfing skills. For easy reference, these drills appear printed in boldface type (as does this passage). The drills are easy to do, and many can be done in a room or in a yard or park. They have helped me with my game and I believe they will help you, too.

At the end of this book you will find an ILLUSTRATED GLOSSARY OF GOLF TERMS. Checking this glossary not only will help you understand golf's special words. It will also clearly illustrate for you the basic mechanical concepts of the golf swing.

2. Rhythm, Balance and Mechanics

A good golf swing can only come about after you have learned the proper way to hold the club and stand up to the ball. A few pages from now, we will discuss these fundamentals of grip and stance.

First, I would like to mention three more general ideas about the golf swing. They are *rhythm*, *balance* and *mechanics*.

These three ideas will help you understand the need for practicing your fundamentals. Also, they will help you decide what changes or improvements to make in the future, whenever you find that your own golf swing is not giving you the results you want.

If you study in this chapter the photos of my swing and of Wayne's, you will see that they do not look exactly alike. That is because our bodies are built differently and have different degrees of flexibility and strength.

These are small differences and they do not make one swing better than the other. The important thing is that both swings have good *rhythm*, *balance* and *mechanics*. They make each swing effective in its own way. They will help make your golf swing effective, too.

Rhythm
The golf swing owes a lot to good rhythm. Anyone who dances or listens to music knows what rhythm or tempo

A balanced finish is a sure sign that a rhythmical swing has been made. Under the pressure of tournament or match play, good rhythm or tempo is especially important.

ADDRESS   **TAKEAWAY**

WINDING UP   **TOP OF SWING**

4

STARTING DOWN   **IMPACT**

FOLLOW-THROUGH   **FINISH**

means. All the great golfers in history had smooth, well-paced swings. This does not mean that all golfers should swing at exactly the same rate. Sam Snead's swing takes a few fractions of a second longer than Arnold Palmer's swing. But each swing obeys its own natural rhythm.

One of the biggest problems for new golfers is rushing or hurrying the swing. That spoils tempo. If you remember that a nice, rhythmical action is the single most important ingredient in your golf game, you will swing the club at the rate of speed that is best for you.

Balance

The golf swing depends a lot on good balance. Some people lose their balance when they swing because they are trying to hit the ball too hard. With practice, good rhythm and good fundamentals will allow you to hit the ball a long way. Consciously "muscling" your shots will not help you gain yardage. If you start and finish your swing in good balance, you won't make that mistake. You will swing within your limits and have a better chance of hitting long and straight shots.

Mechanics

To be useful, a golf swing, like an automobile, must be mechanically sound. Good rhythm, balance and fundamentals will allow you to develop a sound swing that you can repeat over and over without having to think about mechanics. But just as it can be important to the car driver to know what is "under the hood" in an emergency, it may help you as a golfer to know how the good swing works mechanically. Here are the major points.

In a good swing, the club moves like a wheel around the body. The hub of this wheel is in the area of the golfer's neckbone. Think of your arms as the spokes in the wheel.

Your body turns away from the ball and coils like a spring on the backswing. It turns back toward the ball on the downswing and uncoils in time to bring the speeding clubhead into the back of the ball. This clubhead speed is what sends the ball a long way.

When the clubhead meets the ball, the face of the club is looking at the intended target. Another way of saying this is that it is square. This insures accuracy on the shot.

Now that we have in mind these general ideas— rhythm, balance and mechanics—let's pick up a golf club and look at our fundamentals.

3.
Grip and
Stance

Good golf begins with the proper grip. Without the proper grip, you could practice daily and play several times a week—and still never score as well as you should. That's why it's so important to master this fundamental.

The most popular grip is the overlapping grip. In this, the club handle lies diagonally across the palm of the left hand (the right hand for a left-hander). When the right hand is placed next to it on the handle, the little finger of the right hand overlaps the left index finger, piggyback style. This helps the two hands work as a unit.

If you have played baseball or softball, you are familiar with a hitting grip that lacks overlapping. Coming to golf from baseball, you may feel awkward trying to overlap that little finger. When I was first shown this grip, I didn't believe that I would ever be able to hit the ball properly using it. But in time I became comfortable with it. Now I wonder how I ever managed to hit the ball any other way.

To assume the grip properly, stand straight, with hands hanging naturally at your sides. Notice how fingers point to the ground and palms face each other. Bring the hands together in front of you. Don't turn either hand to the right or left as you do so. Now your hands are positioned just as they should be when you place them on the club.

Next, take your club and set it on the ground in front of you, with the handle pointing at your midsection and the face of the club looking squarely at an imaginary target. Place the club handle diagonally across the left palm. It should cross

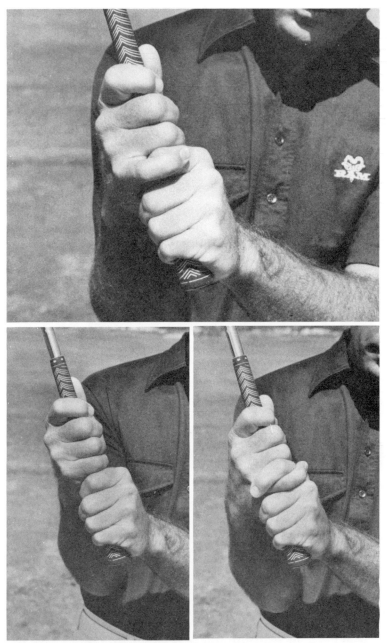

The most popular way to hold the club is in the over-lap grip (above). But the baseball or ten-finger grip (below at left) and the interlock grip also work well, especially for players with smaller or weaker hands.

the palm from a point about one-half inch above the base of the index finger. Then wrap your fingers around the handle, placing your left thumb so it is on top of the handle and pointing straight down.

Place your right hand snugly next to the left. Wrap your fingers around the handle. Let the little finger of the right hand overlap the left index finger.

Many golfers develop swing problems because they turn the hands too far to the right in the grip. This may feel correct because it gives a feeling of strength. But that is misleading. Look down at the "V" formed by the thumb and index finger of each hand as you are gripping the club. If you make sure each "V" is aiming in the direction of your right shoulder, you'll avoid a poor grip.

If your hands are small, you may be able to improve your grip with one small change. Instead of overlapping the left index finger with the right little finger, interlock them. With those two fingers entwined, you may be able to control the club better. When Wayne was beginning golf, he used the interlocking grip with great success. It is a safe and sound method for young people, and also for older players who happen to have small hands. On the pro tour, for example, Jack Nicklaus uses the interlock with great success.

Still another way to hold the club is with a baseball-type grip. Hands are placed together snugly on the handle, with no overlap or interlock. The baseball grip helps the player with very small or weak hands to control the club properly. Again, though, the basic overlapping grip is the one I believe to be most effective.

Whatever grip you decide on, keep the pressure in the grip the same throughout the swing. It's easy to make the mistake of loosening your grip at the top of the backswing, then re-gripping as you start the club down. This fault will throw your club, and your shot, off-line.

Drill for building uniform grip pressure: Line up three balls in front of you, spaced about one foot apart. Take a 6- or 7-iron and address the first ball with the proper grip. Hit the first ball, then immediately step up and hit the second and third balls in succession, without

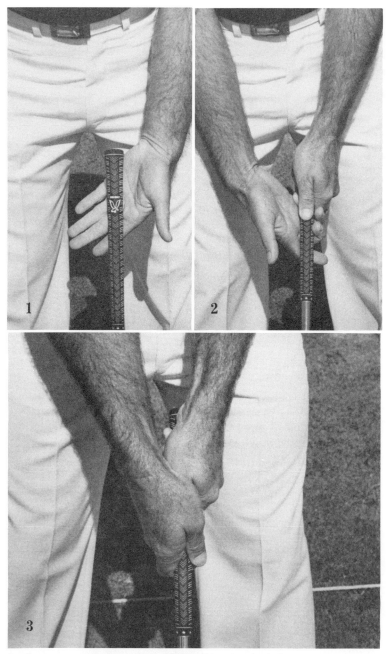

In the proper sequence for building the grip, the left
hand is carefully wrapped around the handle as shown,
then the right hand is fitted snugly next to the left.

taking your hands off the club between shots. You will find that the need to remain in the proper grip for the second and third shots will force you to hold onto the club evenly throughout each swing.

One of the common mistakes that beginners make is gripping too tightly. When there's too much grip pressure, tension builds up in the hands and arms and you can't swing freely or hit the ball very far. Always grip the club lightly. Use only the amount of pressure on the club handle that you use to squeeze toothpaste out of a tube.

Stance

A good stance puts you at just the right distance from the ball to allow you to turn fully on line with your target.

First, let's decide how far apart you should plant your feet. If you take a club in your hands and address the ball, you'll probably take a stance with your feet about as wide apart as your shoulders. That's fine for the driver, or No. 1 wood. Placing the feet any wider would limit your turn. Too narrow a stance causes problems, too, though it's not as common to make that mistake.

When you are using other clubs, especially short irons, you won't need as wide a stance because your swing will not be as full.

It's also best to take what is called a square stance when you're using the driver. That means a line drawn across your toes would be parallel to a line drawn from the ball out to your target. The left foot should be angled a bit to the left, with toes pointing slightly toward the target.

Now let's concentrate on one other important part of the stance—weight distribution.

As you address the ball for a drive, you should feel that about one-third of your weight is on your left side and two-thirds on your right side. It doesn't make sense to have a lot of weight on your left side at address because for a powerful swing, you must transfer weight from the right side to the left side. So the smart thing is to have more of the weight on the right side to begin with.

**Bending the knees slightly at address is one of the
keys to a balanced and comfortable stance.**

31

Drill for proper weight distribution: Take off your right shoe and then address the ball. This automatically lowers your right shoulder and puts more weight on the right side. Take a few practice swings this way and hit some balls, too. Later, when you put your right shoe back on, reproduce the address position you learned in the drill. Now your weight will be distributed properly.

You should also feel your weight more toward the ball of each foot than the heel. If you've played any other sport, you know it is unwise to sit back on your heels when the ball is in play. Instead, you tilt forward slightly, alert and ready to move in any direction. Golf is the same. You must have your weight on the balls of your feet in order to swing fully and freely.

You should also bend your knees slightly. The key word is "slightly." If you are stiff-legged when you swing, you won't hit the ball very far. But golfers sometimes want to bend their knees too much. You only have to bend your knees enough to "unlock" your legs.

4. Full Swing Basics

A track star doesn't walk up to the starting line and then suddenly burst away. He follows a routine that goes by these commands: "On your mark!" "Get set!" "Go!"

Whenever you swing a golf club, whether it's in practice or in play, you should follow a similar routine. It's hard just to step up to the ball and let 'er fly. It's better to go through a pattern that prepares you for the act of striking the ball. This is a hallmark of all good players.

Prepare for your shot by picking out your target. Look at the place where you want your ball to land. Draw a picture in your mind showing the path the ball will fly to get to that spot. Jack Nicklaus never takes a shot in practice or during a tournament without imagining the flight of the ball and the spot where he wants it to come to rest. Jack calls this "going to the movies."

Once you have your shot fixed in your mind's eye, walk up to the ball. Place the clubface behind the ball so it is aimed at your target. Set your grip. Adjust your feet so you're in the proper stance in relation to the ball and your target. Now, with a brief waggle, you're ready to begin the swing.

The Waggle
The waggle is a relaxed movement of the clubhead back and forth above the ball and along the target line just before the backswing begins. It's a way of relieving tension. It also

helps set the proper tempo for the swing.

After the waggle is completed, set the club squarely behind the ball again. The very last thing to do before swinging the club back is to turn your head to the right and fix your attention on the back of the ball with your left or right eye, whichever is stronger or "dominant."

To find out your dominant eye, hold a finger in front of you at eye level. Sight over the tip of the finger toward a fixed object in the distance, such as a doorknob or lightswitch. Close one eye. If your finger seems to jump away from the object you're sighting, then the eye that you closed is your stronger eye. Always use that eye when you sight the ball just before you swing.

2104724

The Takeaway

At the start of the backswing, be very deliberate. Slowly swing the club away from the ball along the ground for about the first foot. Any hurry at all will cause all kinds of problems. In the weeks before the U.S. Open in 1965, I was

Start the club back slowly and smoothly.

rushing my swing badly and knew that if I wanted to be back up among the leaders on tour I was going to have to put the brakes on. Just before I teed off for the first round in the Open, I penciled the word "SLOW" on my golf glove. So every time I looked down at my left hand as I gripped the club for a shot, I was reminded of what I had to do. And I went on to win that tournament, largely because that simple message kept my tempo smooth.

The arms lead the way in the beginning stages of the swing, especially the left arm. Then the shoulders and hips start turning. It's a chain reaction.

Drill to build left arm control: Take your normal stance and grip a 7-iron with the left hand only. Extend your left arm as high as you can on the backswing. Keep head down and elbow straight. Be careful not to turn your body first as you take the club back. It's the left arm that should lead. Pull down with the left arm and swing through.

Top of the Swing

How far back should you take the club? Take as full a swing and as big a turn as you can. Supple players should be able to take the club to a position where it is parallel to the ground and pointing slightly left of your target. Now the club is in excellent position to strike the ball straight and far.

Don't worry if you can't comfortably swing back that far. In fact, if you feel you're over-stretching or are losing control of the club, plan on shortening the backswing enough to make you feel sure of your control.

Here's a good way to make sure you are swinging back to your natural limits. At the instant you've completed the backswing and are about to begin the downswing, your chin should be touching the top of your left shoulder. If you don't feel your chin touching during practice swings, it may mean you would benefit from a bigger turn.

Hands stay firmly on the club at the top.

The Downswing

During the downswing, the clubhead moves with rapidly gathering speed and it is not really possible to control its course after it gets started. That's why your first move on the downswing is so important. Think of starting down with a shift of your weight to the left side. Avoid making your first move with the hands or arms. One easy way to do this is by planting your left heel which was lifted off the ground slightly during the backswing.

Once that heel is planted, your hips will turn to the left and your shoulders, arms and hands will follow in sequence. Again, it's a chain reaction, leading to crisp contact and a full finish.

Don't be afraid of the power you feel building up on the downswing. Try to whip the club through the ball at the fastest speed possible. As long as you keep your left side in control of the swing, it won't hurt you and, in fact, will give you better results.

A drill that helps to develop decisive movement with the left side on the downswing calls for you to stand on your left foot only as you swing a 7-iron. When you do this, you're forced to keep the left side in control on the downswing. If you try to get your right arm or right side involved, you'll lose your balance.

Left side leads the way on the downswing.

The Finish

The idea of hitting *through* the ball is very important. Imagine you're driving a nail into the wall with a hammer. You swing the hammer back and then speed it forward. As you make contact with the nailhead, you don't think of slowing down or stopping the blow. It's the same with the golf club and ball. You are trying to keep the clubhead whizzing along even after the ball has shot off the clubface.

If you have achieved a true swinging action, your weight will have shifted almost entirely onto your left side after you've hit the ball. The momentum of the swing will carry your hands and arms out toward your target and then up high above your left shoulder. Check your finish position to be sure that: 1) your stomach is facing the target; 2) your left leg is straight, and 3) your grip is firm.

The arms, if used like spokes on the wheel, will help you develop your golf swing properly. Your legs can help you, too. For some golfers, this leg action comes naturally. Others can develop it through simple drills, such as this one:

A good way to teach yourself to get your legs into the swing is by means of the one-leg drill. As you address the ball, stand on only your left foot and take your normal swing. Make the drill even more effective by first addressing the ball in your usual way, then hopping from the left foot to the right foot, then hopping back to the left foot and at the same time swinging and hitting the ball. Get as much rhythm into this drill as you can. Once you begin to execute it on "dancing feet," you'll find that your leg action is putting a lot more "zip" in your shots.

Stomach faces target at the finish.

5. Fairway Wood Shots

Golfers have changed their minds about some fairway woods and long irons in recent years. It wasn't long ago that the 2-wood was a standard weapon, used whenever a player wanted to hit the ball as far as possible from off the fairway. Today the 2-wood is rarely used. Clubmaking companies usually don't even include it in their sets. We see few 1-irons around these days, too.

I really can't argue with this change in taste. When I turned professional, the only wood I carried in my bag was a 4-wood. I was going through a stage when I couldn't get the ball up in the air with any of the other woods, including the driver. Hitting with a 4-wood, even off the tee, was the way I solved the problem.

Long irons were also trouble for me when I first began to take golf seriously. Up until I was 16, I never even bothered to carry a 2-iron or 3-iron in my bag.

As I hope this shows, there's no set rule for what clubs you should have in your bag. Carry the ones you like and can do well with. Like many other golfers today, you may prefer a 3-wood, 4-wood or 5-wood over the 2- or 3-iron. If you can hit better shots with those clubs, it makes sense to rely on them.

Hitting With Fairway Woods
To me, the fairway woods represent attacking golf. The 2-wood and 3-wood, because they can send the ball the

In the swing used for the driver or No. 1 wood, the club sweeps the ball off its perch on the tee. Fairway woods are struck with more of a downward blow in order to make the ball rise quickly from its grassy lie.

greatest possible distance from a fairway lie, give you, as no other clubs can, a chance to put the ball on the green on long holes. People don't look upon the 2-wood and 3-wood as stroke savers, but to me that's exactly what they are.

A 3-wood shot off the fairway was the turning point for me in winning the British Open in 1968. The tournament was played at Carnoustie, Scotland that year. I was leading by a stroke as the final round began, but Jack Nicklaus, Billy Casper and Bob Charles were all challenging.

My tee shot on the 14th hole left me 240 yards from the pin. I took out my 3-wood. My view of the green in the distance was blocked by two big bunkers. All I could see was the flag whipping in the strong wind against a backdrop of spectators.

Aiming right at the flag, I hit the ball with so much force that the wind didn't blow it a bit off course. From the moment I swung I had the idea it might be a beauty, and in a couple of seconds the crowd's loud roar told me I was right. My wife, who happened to be in the gallery that day, told me later that when she stood up to clap and saw how close the ball rolled to the hole, her knees buckled and she had to sit right back down again. The birdie I made there gave me a big boost and helped carry me to the title.

I always try to hit my fairway woods with extra enthu-

Keep head down throughout the swing. Jerking the head forward is a common fault when using fairway woods, and results in less-than-solid contact and loss of distance.

siasm. Playing the 15th hole in the 1961 Masters, I slammed a 3-wood shot 245 yards to the 15th green. Actually, this was a case of too much enthusiasm—the ball rocketed over the green. Luckily for me, a spectator standing just in back of the green reached up as if to catch the ball. The ball bounced off his hand and back onto the green.

Both the 3-wood and 4-wood can be used from any decent fairway lie and also from rough if the grass is not too long or thick.

Everything that was said in the previous chapter applies to these clubs. The only difference is that the downswing should be more of a downward blow than it is when you're sweeping the ball off the tee with a driver. The idea is to make the clubface strike the ball just before it reaches the lowest point of its swing arc. When you strike down, you hit the ball up.

To get the most distance with the 3- or 4-wood, be sure not to let your head jerk forward as you swing. This is a common mistake.

Try the "right-leg-only" drill to help you form the habit of staying behind the ball on wood shots from the fairway. Address the ball as usual, but lift your left foot a few inches off the ground, so you're standing completely on your right. Hit several balls this way and you'll quickly improve your arm control and balance.

In using more lofted woods, such as the 5-wood or 6-wood, the swing is the same. But line up so the ball is positioned an inch or so farther back in your stance.

6. Iron Shots

Iron clubs are usually divided up into three categories—long, medium and short. The 1-, 2-, 3- and 4-irons are defined as the long irons. The 5-, 6- and 7-irons are called medium or middle irons. The 8, 9, pitching wedge and sand wedge are the short irons.

The higher the club number, the shorter the shaft and the greater the loft of the clubface. Loft refers to the amount of pitch or slant built into the face. With higher-numbered irons you will get more height on your shots but less distance. The ball will stop fairly quickly after landing. The lower the club number, the longer you can expect your shots to travel, but with less height. The ball will roll farther, after landing.

Irons have grooves etched into the clubface. These grooves help put backspin to the ball. Backspin helps keep the ball flying on a straight lie. Without these grooves, you wouldn't be as accurate with your iron shots. That's why it's a good idea to keep the grooves free of dirt or mud. Use a wooden tee to clear out the grooves when needed.

On the 16th hole, a 405-yard dogleg par 4, I sliced my tee shot, ending up in soggy rough about 150 yards from the green and behind a tall weeping willow tree. The only sensible thing for me to do now appeared to be to chip or pitch back to the fairway, and play for a safe bogey.

I looked things over. I normally hit a 7-iron 150 yards. But in this case, a 7-iron or even an 8-iron would do me no good. Neither club would give any shot enough height to clear the top of the willow tree.

I don't hit a 9-iron 150 yards, but I knew I was charged up and that sometimes makes a person stronger than they normally are. I decided that to stay in contention I would have to go for the green.

Sometimes you have to call upon an iron to do unusual work. In 1972 at the PGA Championship at Oakland Hills in Birmingham, Mich., I was leading by three shots after the third round. But on the final day, I had serious problems. I bogeyed three of the first four holes. On the back nine, I started missing easy putts. It looked as if I were going to drop out of sight.

I pulled the 9-iron from my bag and whacked the ball as hard and as high as I could. Spectators promptly labeled it one of the greatest shots they had ever seen, because the ball ended up four feet from the cup. I made the putt for my birdie, and two holes later I had won the championship.

My main point is, there definitely are times in golf when you can't let yourself be bound by what is normal.

Hitting With Long Irons

The basic difference between the swing used for the 2-, 3-, and 4-irons and the driver swing is that the iron swing is more of a down-and-through stroke. There is somewhat less body turn, because the club shaft is not as long.

To make sure you strike the ball before the club has reached the bottom of its swing arc, position the ball a couple of inches farther back from the front foot in your stance. This in turn helps you to maintain a down-and-through striking action in the stroke.

A couple of other points about long irons deserve special mention. When hitting a long-iron shot, you will pick up the club a bit more on the backswing, as opposed to sweeping it back as fully as you do with a wood. During the downswing, you may also feel that you are shifting your weight to the left side more readily. This is natural and will not affect your shot provided you have made a full shoulder turn. Just make sure the clubface strikes the back of the ball before it hits the

The ball is placed farther back in the stance for iron shots. On the backswing you may feel as if you are picking up the club a bit more, as opposed to sweeping it back as fully as you do with a wood club.

turf, as this is the type of contact that will get the ball into the air.

If your ball is sitting up nicely in the fairway, you may be able to sweep the club through impact without taking a divot—unless you have failed to meet the ball before the bottom of your swing arc. Generally, the shorter the iron, the bigger the divot you should take. (Good etiquette requires that you replace every chunk of sod you take with your shots—it helps keep golf courses green.)

If you're having trouble shifting your weight with your long-iron swing, check your stance. Your feet may be too wide apart. Try placing them a bit closer together. It will be easier for your weight to turn and return during the swing.

3

4

If your long-iron swing feels out of control to you, grip down on the handle about an inch from the butt end. This shortens the club and permits you to make a more compact swing.

Many young players worry about being able to get the ball into the air with the long irons because the clubface has so little loft. They develop a kind of scooping action as a result, which might creep into all their other shots, too. A good mental drill to overcome this fear is to make believe you have a 9-iron in your hands when you're hitting with a long iron. This may help you bring forth a smooth, well-paced swing right away.

Hitting With the Medium and Short Irons

A descending blow should also be used in the swing for the middle irons (5-, 6- and 7-irons) and the short irons (8- and 9-irons and wedge). Two important adjustments in stance will allow you to hit short and middle irons crisply.

First, place your feet closer together as you address the ball. The shorter shafts on the clubs automatically reduce the arc of your swing and the need to make a full body turn.

Second, draw your left foot back an inch or two from the target line so you are in a slightly open, instead of a square, stance. This will reduce your body action slightly and improve the accuracy of your swing.

7

8

The downswing with an iron is a descending blow.
The idea is to meet the ball just before the club
reaches the bottom of its swing arc. The loft of the
clubface itself will insure that the ball flies up
quickly.

Take the club back low along the ground, but allow it to
swing upward a bit sooner. The downswing should begin
slowly and deliberately, but the shift of weight back to the
left side should be made without delay. This helps you generate more of a down-and-through stroke.

A good drill to develop proper timing is to take a
5-iron and hit four or five shots in a row, making each shot
travel no farther than one of your 7-iron shots. Limiting
your distance will cause you to slow the pace of your
swing and improve your timing.

7.
Short
Game
Shots

Frequently, you will find your ball too near the green to make a full swing with any club, yet not close enough to putt. That is when you must employ a less-than-full swing to produce chip shots or pitch shots.

Chip shots are usually played from within 25 yards of the green. They are played with less-lofted clubs such as the 5-, 6- or 7-iron. The ball flies low, lands a few feet on the green and rolls to the hole.

Pitch shots are usually played with wedges. They fly higher than chip shots and come to rest quickly after landing on the green.

Since most golfers take more "mini-strokes" than full-swing strokes during a round, learning short game skills well is a sure way to lower your scores quickly.

Suppose your drive and fairway shots leave you 40 yards from the cup on a certain hole? Most players figure to get down in three strokes from that distance—a pitch shot to the green and two putts. But if you're clever with your short-game clubs, you may be able to drop the ball close to the pin and hole out with one putt.

This is exactly what happened to me in the Masters Tournament in 1974. Playing the 71st hole, I was leading Dave Stockton by a stroke. My 9-iron approach shot to the green stopped five inches beyond the cup. When I holed out for my birdie, I had a two-stroke lead. That took the pressure off me and I was able to play the last hole with great confidence.

**The chip shot from off the green is made with a
greatly reduced swing using upper body and arms,
with no real body turn or weight shift.**

Chipping

When you're within 25 yards of the green, chipping is usually
the best way to get the ball near the hole. One exception
would be when there's a bunker or some other hazard between the ball and the hole. In this case, you would hit a pitch
shot to keep the ball aloft and so avoid rolling into trouble.

Another exception would be when your ball is just off
the green, resting on the short fringe grass. Here it's almost
always better to use your putter.

The chip shot is made with a reduced swing using the
upper body and arms. There is no real body turn or weight
shift. Imagine you're tossing a ball to a friend who is only 10
or 15 yards away. You wouldn't wind up to make the throw.
You wouldn't use much leg action. You'd simply swing your
arm and toss the ball. Think of the chip shot the same way.

When chipping, use a less-lofted club, such as the 7-

iron. Plan to land the ball on the green just beyond the fringe, allowing for it to roll the rest of the way to the cup. If you aimed too near the cup, chances are the ball would roll too far past.

Open your stance so the left foot is farther back from the target line than the right. Be careful not to draw your left shoulder and hip back at the same time. That could cause you to cut across the ball.

Play the ball from the center of your stance—at a spot the same distance from each foot. When I'm chipping, I like to feel that my left foot is nailed to the ground and that all my weight is concentrated on it. The left side becomes the brace for my swing.

A short, smooth backswing is all that's required for the chip shot. It's vital that your hands lead the club on the downswing. This assures you'll hit down on the ball. If your hands don't lead, you're almost certain to mis-hit the ball.

A good drill to develop the feel of chip shots is to take a 7-iron in your left hand and hit six or seven balls in succession. Chipping with only the left arm helps you build a crisp downward striking action.

Pitching

The best clubs for pitching are the 9-iron and pitching wedge or even the sand wedge, which many of my fellow pros use on tour. With these you can send the ball high into the air and make it bite—stop quickly on the green near the pin. The wedges are better suited than the 9-iron because of their design. They feature a highly lofted face and a flanged sole that keeps the club from digging too deeply into the turf. If you own a wedge and practice with it enough, you will be able to pitch the ball with great accuracy from any distance from 25 up to 100 yards.

Some players have trouble playing pitch shots because they overpower them. A big, sweeping swing isn't called for when you're pitching or chipping. You want a short, controlled swing that will put the ball close to the hole.

The pitching stroke differs from the chip in several ways. You must play the ball at a point closer to your left heel. Your weight should be more on the right foot at address. There is more arm motion in the swing itself. Try taking the club back until your left arm is about parallel to the ground. This backswing will give you time to shift your weight to the left side as the arms swing the club through. As you practice this shot, you will find that by taking the club back a little more or a little less than normal will help you produce shots of varying distances.

A good mental drill for improving pitch shot accuracy is to make the top of the flagpole on the green your aiming point. Most players are short with their pitch shots, chiefly because they use the hole as their target and overestimate the amount of roll they will get. If you aim for the top of the pole, you're more likely to drop the ball within "short-putt" range.

Unlike the chip, the pitch shot flies high, stops quickly after it lands. The location of your ball in relation to the green dictates whether you should chip or pitch.

8. Putting

The putting stroke is short and simple and takes hardly any physical strength. It is one part of the game in which young people can compete on a level with more experienced golfers right from the start.

In one way, younger players have a big advantage on the greens. They are unafraid of missing putts. Adults tend to be much more cautious and even fearful. They have more three-putt greens than they really should have.

This is not to say that you should take your putting less seriously than any other part of your game. About half of the strokes that go into the total score for a typical round are putts. So even when a putt is only a foot or so in length, be deliberate. You'll never see me raking a putt into the hole or slapping at one with a quick or casual stroke. At one tour event in 1978, Bruce Lietzke tried a backhanded putt on an early hole and missed it. He ended the tournament tied for the lead and lost in a playoff.

The moral is: Treat every putt with respect.

Putting Styles

You'll see all kinds of putting styles on the greens. I once knew a South African who putted with his hands reversed on the handle, his right hand above his left. He was a splendid putter. Another golfer I once knew putted between his legs. He wasn't bad either! Sam Snead has been effective in recent years putting "sidesaddle"—with one hand high on the club handle and the other low on the shaft.

My own style involves a jab-type stroke. I developed it when I first started playing professional golf in the United States. That was in 1957. Billy Casper, Doug Ford, and the other outstanding putters of that period were jab putters and I copied them.

With a jab stroke, you stand in a narrow, closed stance and kind of punch the ball, giving it a rap. There's a good deal of wrist action and very little follow-through. Some people say it's more of a chipping stroke than a putting stroke.

I can't honestly recommend the jab style to most golfers. It has too many variables.

The style I do recommend is the one Wayne uses. It is also the style used by almost all of today's top pros. It is popular because it is less prone to human error.

In this style, your feet are planted 14 or 15 inches apart. The stance is square or slightly open to the target line. Weight is evenly distributed. The stroke itself is made with arms and shoulders, not wrists.

The putter is used as an extension of your left arm. The distance the putt rolls and the speed the ball travels are controlled by the swing of the left arm. The blade of the putter stays square to the target line. After the ball is struck, the blade keeps moving smoothly along the target line a short distance.

How you grip the putter is a matter of personal preference. But it makes sense to keep the grip the same or very similar to your normal grip. The less grip-changing required as you go from fairway to green, the better off you'll be. Always grip a putter lightly, for your best possible "touch," and keep the light pressure on the handle the same from the beginning of the stroke to the end.

Where you place your hands on the handle varies somewhat according to the length of putt you have. For short putts, crouch more and grip farther down the handle. For long putts, stand more erect and take your grip more toward the butt end.

No matter how long or short the putt is, it's important to stand close enough to the ball so you can look straight down

There are many different putting styles, but the most reliable stroke is one being used here by Wayne. The putter is swung in a pendulum motion using arms and shoulders, but not wrists.

at it as you get set to stroke. You should be able to draw a line straight down from your left eye to the ball.

After any putt is struck, it's a good idea to keep your eyes down and your head still for a moment, rather than to look up right away to see where the ball is going. This will help you build smoothness in your stroke.

Be sure to strike the ball at the same spot on your putter blade every time. Some putters have this "sweet spot" marked on the top with a line, so that you can be sure you are lining up blade and ball correctly.

Lining Up Straight Putts

On short putts, make your target the back edge of the hole.

Line up with that target and plan to stroke the ball straight at it.

On longer putts, pick out a spot on your target line, about 12–14 inches from the ball. When you putt, roll the ball over the spot. If your overall line is correct, the ball will head for the cup.

When you're faced with a very long putt, imagine the hole to be the bull's-eye of a target that's three or four feet in diameter. Make it your goal to place the ball within that target area on the first putt. Then you can safely go for the bull's-eye with your second putt.

Lining Up Breaking Putts

Generally, short putts of less than six feet can be played as straight putts. On longer putts the slope, speed and often the grain of the green must be checked before deciding where you are going to aim your putt or how firmly you are going to hit it.

Slope is the way a green pitches in relation to surrounding ground. The best way to see slope is to study the green as you walk to it from the fairway. It's harder to get a good picture of slope standing on the green.

Speed refers to how quickly the ball will roll because of the condition of the putting surface itself. If the grass is closely trimmed and the soil dry and hard packed, the green is fast and the ball will roll easily. If the grass has not been trimmed in the past 24 hours, or has been watered recently, the green will be slow. It will take a firmer stroke to get the ball to the hole.

On courses in some parts of the country, grass on greens grows visibly in a specific direction. This is known as grain and it, too, can affect your putts. Stand behind your ball and look toward the hole. If the grass appears shiny, it is growing away from you. This will make the ball roll more, so you'll have to use a lighter touch on your stroke. If you can't see any shine, the grass is growing toward you. You'll be putting against the grain, so you'll have to be a bit bolder.

When you play on a course that is new to you, take long

practice putts. They will give you a good picture of how the greens break and whether they are fast or slow. You can't learn nearly as much about the greens from short practice putts.

A good drill for accurate putting is to line up six balls along an imaginary line extending outward from the hole. Place the first ball one foot from the hole; the second, two feet from the hole; the third, three feet, and so on. Sink the one-footer first, then the two-footer, etc., finishing with the six-footer. Anytime you miss one of the putts, you must begin again. Make up your mind that you're going to do this drill successfully five times before you leave the green.

Confidence

I've always been a good putter, even though, as I said before, I do not think my putting style is one that should be copied. My confidence in my putting has been so great that I think it has made up for any technical shortcomings.

One of the tricks that helps me feel sure of myself on the greens is that when I'm getting set to stroke, I always picture the ball going right into the hole. I hold that image in my mind as I bend over the ball and even when I take the putter back. And that's what you should train yourself to do. If you can't "see" the ball going in before your stroke, it's very likely that it's not going to drop for you.

I think Arnold Palmer's lack of success as a putter during the mid- to late 1970s could be blamed on his loss of confidence more than anything else. During the 1960s, there was no putter in the world better than Arnold. I remember how bold he was on the greens. He'd step up to the ball and really swat it, often sending it three or four feet past the hole. Then he'd sink it on the way back. He was never short with his first putt. He always gave it a chance to go in the hole.

Tom Watson and Andy Bean are about the best putters among today's top golfers. Bean has a marvelous touch for someone who is 6 feet 4 inches tall and weighs more than 200 pounds. I feel Watson has to be ranked higher because of what he's accomplished. In 1977, 1978 and 1979 he was the leading money winner on the golf tour, and you don't do that without being a fantastic putter.

I think practice was the major factor in the development of Watson's great putting. When Tom was a youngster growing up in Kansas City, he enjoyed playing golf, but he was often short on golf balls and couldn't always afford to buy new ones. So he devoted a lot of his time to putting and chipping, because he didn't have to worry about losing any balls that way.

9. Trouble Shots

At the famous Old Course in St. Andrews, Scotland, there's a tar roadway that cuts through the 18th fairway. Thousands of golfers have had to play their second shots from this unyielding surface. Ordinarily, the remaining distance to the green from this place would call for a 9-iron.

Most golfers react to a lie on a tar roadway with panic. Their fear of the shot creates so much tension in them that they never make a good stroke.

If you were faced with this shot, here's what I would tell you: Relax. Forget the hard surface. Play your normal 9-iron shot. If you do so, there's a good chance you'll be on the green.

What I'm suggesting is that if you step up to a ball in a poor lie, don't fret about it and just make your normal swing, it's very likely you will get normal results.

So my first rule for playing trouble shots is: *Focus on only the good things that are going to happen.* You must be positive even though you may be faced with what looks like a catastrophe.

My second rule is: *Bear down more.* Special shots demand special attention. Imagine you're playing the final round in the World Series of Golf, with millions watching on television and your family waiting for you at the 18th green. You need a good shot to hold your one-stroke lead. If you get your adrenalin flowing, you'll be surprised how often and easily you get out of trouble.

Rule No. 3: *When in trouble, use your imagination.*

Look at all the possible shots you could play to get back into contention.

Let me set up this situation for you: You've hit your second shot on a par-4 hole and it slanted to the left, bounced a few times, and rolled up close to a trench-like bunker that's 30 yards from the green. The ball is so close to the gully that there's no room to stand and swing. And you can't address the ball in the ditch because it's too deep. The ball would be at about belt level if you tried.

Some people would try to play this shot left-handed, and they'd probably flub it. As soon as you attempt taking very much of a backswing from the "wrong" side, you're in trouble. You simply can't keep the club on the proper track.

Here's a more unusual way to play this shot, and I think a safer way. Stand with your *back* to the hole and line up the ball with the flag by peering through your legs. Now lift the club straight up in front of you, then swing down and through your legs. It's almost the same stroke you would use when chopping wood and doesn't feel nearly as awkward as when you try to swing left-handed. You can generate a good deal of power with this makeshift stroke, so hitting 30 yards to the green would be a cinch.

Confidence, concentration and imagination—those three qualities will help you master all sorts of trouble shots in golf.

From the Sand

A shot out of the sand should be no more of a problem than a drive or fairway shot. I keep a record of how I fare with my bunker shots. During one recent sequence of 72 times in bunkers, I got up and down in two shots 64 times, in three shots only once, and I holed out the other seven times. There's no reason you can't develop percentages that approach these.

You can use a pitching wedge in hitting out of traps, but a sand wedge works even better and is well worth the cost. The two clubs are about the same, but the sand wedge has a wider flange on the bottom so it slips through more easily.

When you address the ball in a bunker, wriggle your feet back and forth until your shoes are partially buried in the sand. Digging in like this will assure you a firm footing. It also helps you determine the texture of the sand—whether it is dry and loose or wet and firm. The firmer the sand, the farther your ball will travel, so a shorter swing is dictated.

I hit just about every bunker shot with the same tempo, and you should try to do this, too, whether you want the ball to go 5 yards or 25 yards. What changes is the *amount* of sand you take with the shot. For a shot that's only a few yards long, you should hit three inches behind the ball. The farther you want the ball to go, the less sand you take. For a 25-yarder, I might hit only an inch behind the ball.

Where you position the ball in your stance is very important. For a bunker shot of 20 or 25 yards, spot the ball at about the center of your stance. If the shot is shorter, line the ball up more toward your left heel. That way the club-

The key to escaping from sand with control is to hit 1″–3″ behind the ball, using the sand itself to pop the ball out. The farther you want the ball to go, the less sand you take.

head will skim through the sand at less of an angle and plop the ball the shorter distance required.

Choke up on the club an inch or so on bunker shots. It will give you a more controlled feeling. Be sure to hit through the ball—if you leave the club in the sand, you can be sure the ball will stay in the sand, too.

When the ball is buried in a trap, special tactics are required. It's worth learning these tactics because the machinery used to maintain bunkers today tends to render the sand soft and powdery. As a result, buried lies are much more common.

Use almost a square stance, and spot the ball in the center of your stance. Use your hands to lead the club into the ball. This will close the clubface at impact. Hit two inches behind the ball and shorten your follow-through. The ball will pop out of the sand with little or no backspin. Try to allow for the ball to run more after it hits the green.

To me and most other tour professionals, the hardest shot in golf is the 60- to 70-yard approach shot out of a bunker. Instead of a sand wedge, try a 9-iron or an 8-iron. To make the ball fly fairly low so it covers the required distance, lead the downswing with your hands so the clubface is slightly closed as you swing through. Again, be sure to follow through.

This drill will give you a feeling for sand shots and how the ball should behave. During a practice round, toss a ball into a trap. Now go in after it, pick it up, then toss the ball underhanded toward the cup—just as if you were trying to hole it. Then, using a second ball from the same spot, try hitting out with your wedge. Your shot should produce about the same trajectory as the ball you tossed out. Continue to practice, tossing one ball, hitting a second one, at other bunkers throughout the round.

From the Rough
The hardest shots of all usually come when your ball leaves the fairway. The term rough usually refers to the area that

**When your ball is off the fairway in heavy grass or
rough, make sure to swing through the ball with
extra firmness—and don't expect pinpoint accuracy
on the shot.**

borders the fairway where tall and thick grass grows, but rough can also be made of thornbushes, rock- or gravel-strewn ground, or even swampland. In other words, any type of wild, unfriendly land.

When your ball is in rough of any kind, don't think in terms of sending it soaring over trees and hazards and landing it on the green. Shots from the rough are hard to control, so it's poor strategy to depend on pinpoint accuracy with them.

In most lies from thick grass, the ball is propped up somewhat by the grass. This means your club will put less backspin on the shot. Because the ball will therefore run farther, you should use one club less than you normally would from that distance.

Play the ball a bit farther back in your stance than would be normal for the club you are using. This will ensure that the clubhead contacts the ball, not the grass, first.

Make sure you swing through the ball and finish well on any shot from rough. Not quitting on the shot is extremely important. I remember playing in a British Open with Arnold Palmer some years ago when Arnold saw his tee shot end up in a stand of thick heather. It didn't bother him. Using a 6-iron, he unleashed a ferocious swing at a ball he could scarcely see. Clumps of grass and branches of heather went flying through the air, but the ball landed on the green.

Even though you do swing firmly, there is always a chance that long grass will get in the way and turn the clubhead in your hands. This usually causes the ball to veer to the left. But you can adjust for this by opening up your stance—drawing your left foot back—and aiming slightly to the right of your target. The longer the rough, the more important it is to make this adjustment.

When the grass is very long and thick, it can also get in the way of your clubhead on the backswing. Instead of keeping the clubhead low as you take it back, you may have to pick it up somewhat sharply, so you will tend to chop down on the ball. But if you make sure to follow through, you will still produce an escape.

If the ball is buried deep in the grass, your best play is simply to take a wedge and hit it back to the fairway as near to the hole as possible. That is a much better choice than trying a near-impossible shot and remaining in the rough.

Uneven Lies

On a course laid out over hilly terrain, you will often find your ball on down-slopes, up-slopes, or side-slopes. These hilly lies call for special techniques.

Suppose the ball is in a downhill lie. Because this type of lie tends to increase the distance you'll get, select one club less than normal for the job. Play the ball more toward the back of your stance. At address, your left foot will be lower than your right, so take care not to shift your weight forward too soon. Otherwise, your hands will get too far ahead of the clubhead and push the shot to the right.

In playing from a sidehill lie, with ball below feet, it's vital to "sit back" on your heels during swing.

In an uphill lie, the opposite strategy applies. Now your right foot is on a lower level than your left. This makes it harder to shift weight back to the left side as you begin the downswing, so put extra weight on the left side at address. Position the ball a bit more forward in your stance. Select a less-lofted club to compensate for the fact that the shot will fly higher than normal from this type of lie.

Sidehill lies come in two varieties. In one, the ball is below your feet. In this case, you must make a special effort to keep weight back on your heels as you swing. Because you'll be more upright as you swing, there'll be a tendency to push the ball to the right. Compensate for this by aiming several yards to the left of your actual target.

In the case of a ball that is higher than your feet, the tendency will be to pull the ball to the left, so this time aim a bit right of your actual target. Stand farther from the ball at address and concentrate on keeping your weight forward.

From a Divot Mark

Once in a while you will hit a good shot and smile in satisfaction, but when you reach the ball you find it resting in a divot hole. Don't get upset. Keep your hands out in front as you swing. This assures that you'll hit the ball, not the ground, first. What you're really doing is forcing the ball out of its hole and sending it away on a low trajectory.

Wind and Weather

Here are some tips on trouble shots you are likely to face when you are playing in unusual weather conditions.

A lot of rain means soggy fairways. When these conditions exist, you're not going to get any roll with your drives. The ball will plunk down and stop dead, so you should make a greater effort to keep the ball up in the air longer. Tee up your drives higher than normal when the fairways are soft. This will keep your ball high. Doing this, I figure I add 10 to 15 yards to my drives.

Playing into greens in rainy conditions may dictate a

change in club selection. Allow for more run (even though the wet greens hold better) and use one less club than normal. This should be done in the early morning hours, too, when fairways and greens are blanketed with dew.

When playing a short or medium iron into a green when there's a strong headwind blowing, use one more club than you would normally. If it's a normal 7-iron shot, use a 6-iron. This makes up for what the wind is going to do to the ball's flight. I sometimes draw an imaginary green in front of the actual green and play for *it*. The ball hits down on or just in front of the "real" green, and bounds toward the hole.

Conversely, when playing this same hole downwind, you would take a 7-iron instead of a 6-iron.

Should you face a crosswind on an iron shot to the green, adjust by using one more club than usual and hitting at less than full power. In a normal 6-iron situation, use a 5-iron or maybe even a 4-iron. What you're trying to do is keep the ball low, out of the wind.

Try not to let extremes in temperature bother you. When it's hot and humid, make up your mind to pace yourself so you don't become tired on the finishing holes. Rest while your opponents are shooting. Drink plenty of water early in the day—don't wait until you begin to get thirsty. Be sure to wear a lightweight, peaked hat to keep the sun off your head and out of your eyes. Many golfers prefer to go hatless, but I think they are taking an unnecessary risk. On very hot days, I carry a towel and wet half of it, then put it around my neck as I'm walking down the fairway. I'll also wear a hat that I have deliberately soaked in water. I once played in a tournament in the Philippines, where it can be broiling in the sun. Some local golfers showed me how to stuff my hat with green leaves, which they said would absorb the heat. It worked pretty well!

When playing in cold weather, be sure to dress properly. On very cold days, I wear two pairs of socks and thermal underwear. I cut off the sleeves of the thermals at the shoulders so I'm able to swing freely. I also may wear a thermal vest under a loose-fitting wool sweater. I wear a wool hat that covers my ears. Between shots, I put on mittens, and also I carry a hand warmer in my pocket.

10. Tactics on the Course

At the Glen Abbey Golf Course in Oakville, Ontario, frequently the scene of the Canadian Open, there's a 506-yard, par-5 hole that I play in an unusual way. It's unusual because I don't use a driver.

A wide creek crosses the narrow, windswept fairway just beyond the tee, and doubles back to cut through the fairway again in front of the green. My idea in playing the hole is to use a 1-iron off the tee and follow with a 3-iron from the fairway. This brings me to a point just in front of the creek; it's then a short pitch to the green.

Using a driver wouldn't help me. I'd still have a risky second shot—I'd be as likely to put the ball in the creek as on the green. With the driver, I'd still have to lay up short of the water with my second shot, probably using a 5-iron.

In other words, the driver and 5-iron bring me to exactly the same spot as using a 1-iron and a 3-iron. The advantage of using the 1-iron is that I can be more accurate. When danger increases with distance, I always say that the best thing to do with the driver is to leave it in your bag.

Strategic planning of this sort depends on knowing accurately two kinds of information:

How far you hit the ball with each club in your bag. These yardages you can figure out simply by pacing off several typical shots with each of your clubs and coming in with an average length for each club.

How far you are from your targets on the course. Today's pros and their caddies make it a point to measure

Knowing exactly how far you are from your targets
on the course will help you choose the right clubs for
your shots. One of the things serious golfers do in
preparing for a tournament is to make up a notebook
with all the pertinent yardages written down.

carefully the distance from various points on the fairway to the green.

This careful approach to the game is of recent origin. It's one reason that golfers today are scoring better than golfers of a decade or two ago. When you have such information, you can be certain you're using the right club every time you swing.

Determining your own yardages and learning to figure out the distances from various spots on the course are only two important parts of this thinking man's game called golf. In this chapter, I want to point out some of the other ways in which using your head to manage your talent can lead to lower scores.

Gear Yourself to Play Your Best
Preparation for a round of golf should begin before you step onto the first tee. Try to arrive at the course in enough time to warm up. Start by hitting short iron shots, then work up through the medium and long irons to the woods. Take a few swings with each club. Not only are you loosening your muscles, but you're grooving your swing. Finish the warm-up session with some practice putting.

When you walk to the first tee, gear yourself up mentally. Make up your mind that you are going to begin well. Some golfers play three or four holes before they start to concentrate. By then they may have hit five or six careless shots.

Shoot For a Number on Every Hole
As you play each hole, have a goal in mind. When I'm playing my best, my aim is to birdie every hole. But be realistic. If you're not yet long off the tee and don't have much luck with fairway woods or long irons, why try to reach the green of a 417-yard, par-4 hole in two shots? A par is not a realistic goal for you on such a hole, so instead set either four, five or six strokes as your goal. If you can get down in the figure you are shooting for, you have succeeded.

72

Play Your Tee Shots Away From Trouble

Before you tee off, check which side of the fairway has more troubles. If there's an out-of-bounds area on the left side, tee up on the left-hand side of the tee. You'll be more likely to shoot away from trouble, not toward it.

Pick the Most Favorable Landing Area

Always play your drive so that it puts you where you can hit an open shot to the green. Sometimes hazards near the green may dictate your choice. Take the 11th hole at Augusta National. Most golfers drive down the right side of the fairway, which leaves them with a 5-iron or 6-iron shot to the green. But there are water hazards beyond and to the left of the green. And because the fairway slopes from right to left, it's not hard to hook the ball and end up in the water. So my strategy has always been to play down the left side. It's a longer route and leaves me with a 4-iron for my second shot, but I feel it's smarter to go that way.

Aim Approach Shots According to Pin Positions and Slope of Green

When you are playing to a green where the flag is far to the left or right, with bunkers or any other trouble around, aim for the middle of the putting surface. If you're skilled enough, you can draw or fade the ball, but your target should still be the center of the green.

If the flag is in the center of a green that slopes toward you, play for the front part of the green. This will give you an uphill putt, which is easier to make than a downhill putt.

When the flag is in the center of a flat green, play for the back of the green, using one more club than you normally would, if need be. The reason for this is that most golfers play for the front of a green. So that area becomes worn and pocked with spike marks, and harder to putt than the back part of the green.

When you do put an approach shot onto the green,

immediately return your iron to the bag and take out your putter. As you walk to the green, you'll have more time to get used to the putter's weight and feel.

When Necessary, Fade or Draw Your Shot

The best golfers are those who can maneuver the ball when the course layout or conditions demand this. For instance, on a fairway that slopes from left to right, I usually try to draw the ball—make it curve slightly from right to left—especially if there's a bunker or water hazard on the right side of the fairway.

To draw the ball, close your stance by drawing your right foot back a couple of inches from the target line. Take the club back more inside that line than normal. When you swing through, the club should travel on an inside-to-outside path, with the right hand rolling over the left during impact, imparting a counterclockwise spin to the ball, which produces the draw.

To fade the ball—make it curve slightly from left to right—open your stance by drawing your left foot back from the target line. Take the club back outside that line. On the downswing, the club will travel from outside to inside, cutting across the ball. This imparts a clockwise spin and the fade.

Tee Your Ball on All Par-3's

One of golfing's myths is that not teeing up on short par-3 holes will help you add backspin to your shot. Actually, when you don't tee up, there's more of a tendency to hit behind the ball, which would result in less backspin. Tee up on every short hole. You're much more likely to hit the ball first and so get *increased* backspin.

Fight Fatigue by Swinging Easier With Longer Clubs

If you begin to feel tired toward the end of a round, don't do as many young players do and try to hit each shot harder. Do

74

just the opposite. Aching or tired muscles are telling you they want to do less work, not more. So shorten your backswing and swing more easily. Use one more club so you can cover the distance you need without strain.

Take the Tournaments You Enter Seriously

Competition can't help but sharpen your skills, so enter local or club tournaments whenever you have a chance. But prepare yourself by scouting the tournament site and practicing as much as you can. Decide how you're going to play each hole on the course and then work on the shots that your tactics call for. Before I go to the Masters each year, I practice drawing the ball a lot, because that's the shot best suited to the fairways at Augusta.

When playing a practice round, try to visualize the various spots on each green where the pin is likely to be placed during the tournament. Then putt for each of those spots, looking for unusual break or speed. That way, during the tournament, no pin placements will take you by surprise.

One last bit of advice: Never give up. Even after a bad shot or a bad hole, keep concentrating. Forget what happened. Otherwise, you'll get careless and start wasting shots.

At the 1978 Masters I began the final round seven shots behind Hubie Green, the leader. Even so, I was bursting with confidence. I remember telling my caddie I thought I had a good chance to win.

I got away fast with a birdie 4 on the second hole, and on the par-3 fourth sank a big 30-footer for another birdie. I had trouble on the seventh, coming out of a bunker to within five feet of the cup, then missing the putt for a bogey. But after I birdied the ninth, I had a 34 for the first nine holes. Hubie was to have a 36. I wasn't making great progress, but I was still charged up.

As the second nine began, I started making up ground quickly. I sank birdie putts of 25 feet on the 10th hole and 15 feet on the 12th. I birdied the 13th and 15th. When I sank a 14-foot birdie putt on the 16th, the standings board showed that I was 10 under par and tied for the lead. On the 18th, I hit a 6-iron that put me 15 feet from the cup and then I curled it in for my seventh birdie in 10 holes. I ended with a 64 for the day—a record held by only four others—and a one-shot lead.

Green, Tom Watson and Rod Funseth all had a chance to tie me and force a playoff. One by one they came to the 18th green—and failed.

It marked the third time I had won at Augusta. But if I had quit, the tournament would have belonged to someone else.

Try to do your best every minute you're out on the course. The results may surprise you.

11. Golf Etiquette

The Rules of Golf as set down by the United States Golf Association (USGA) and the Royal and Ancient Golf Club of St. Andrews (R & A, the organization that governs golf in Great Britain) cover just about every situation you'll ever run into on the course. These rules aren't meant to limit your enjoyment of the game in any way. They merely express those laws of play that generations of golfers have found to be the fairest for all. They are clearly stated in a pocket-sized booklet available for 50¢ from the USGA, Far Hills, N.J., 07931. A serious golfer will want a copy of the rules to read and keep in his or her golf bag.

In this chapter, I want to discuss not rules but etiquette —the courtesies that good golfers show to one another on the course. When they're observed by everyone, everyone enjoys golf that much more.

1. "Players should play without delay" is undoubtedly the simplest of all the rules of etiquette, but it's probably the one most violated. I think that professional golfers may be at fault here. When competing in important tournaments for enormous sums of money, they often do take too much time, especially on the greens.

I'm not urging you to hurry your shots, but please always do make an effort to play with deliberate speed. Always be ready to hit when it's your turn. Step up to the ball, pick out your target, get yourself set, and swing. On the greens, do line up every putt, but don't take more time than is absolutely needed to do so.

Here are the other important rules of etiquette you should know:

2. Begin your golfing day by arriving at the first tee at the agreed-upon time, ready to play.

3. Observe the proper order of play. At the first tee, the amateur golfer with the lowest handicap usually hits first. Pros usually flip a coin to decide. On subsequent holes, the right to hit first goes to the player having the lowest score on the previous hole. Once the player has gained the honor, he keeps it until another player plays a hole in fewer strokes.

4. Never shoot until you have checked to see that players in front of you on the course are well out of range.

5. Do not distract or disturb another player while he or she is shooting. Don't stand in that player's line of vision, including directly behind the player.

6. Let faster groups play through. If a ball veers into the rough and you realize you will have to spend several minutes looking for it, allow the players behind you to play through. Once you've signaled them, you and the other members of your group should keep to the sides of the fairway until the other group has gone by.

7. Take care of the golf course. When you shoot from a fairway and take a divot, be sure to replace it, pressing it down firmly with your spikes so that the turf will re-root. When you shoot from a bunker, rake and smooth out the depressions made by clubhead and feet. Never drop your bag on a green. Never pull a cart onto a green. When you remove the flagstick, be careful not to damage the green with it. Repair ball marks and spike marks on the green, not only your own but any you happen to come upon. To repair a ball mark, probe under the depression with a tee, pressing down so the tip lifts the turf to normal level. If everyone followed this rule, putts would roll truer.

8. Once you've completed play on a hole, replace the flagstick and leave the green immediately. Don't stand around talking about your putts or writing down the scores —do that on the way to the next tee.

Treat all players, regardless of age, sex or ability, with courtesy.

12.
Exercise
and
Diet

I have long felt that physical fitness is important for golfers
of every age and condition. To build up my legs, I've skipped
rope hour after hour and done half-squats by the hundreds. I
used to do a slew of fingertip pushups every day. Long
before jogging became popular, I was running two or three
miles a day four or five times a week.

Part of my enthusiasm to be well-muscled and physical-
ly fit stems from my size—or lack of it. I am 5 feet 7 inches
tall and weigh 150 pounds. During my early years as a
professional, some people said that I wasn't big enough to be
a really top-flight golfer. Such comments only drove me to
adopt a tough exercise program and to practice harder.

While I don't recommend that you follow an exercise
program as intensive as mine, you do have to maintain a
certain level of fitness to play your best golf. It takes physical strength to execute the shots a round of golf demands. It
takes stamina to withstand physical and mental fatigue in
the final stages of a round.

In this chapter I would like to share some of my
thoughts on fitness and health and suggest for those who are
interested a number of physical routines that can directly
benefit your golf.

Running
Of all the sports and activities you may engage in, none is

better for good physical fitness than running. It can be almost any kind of running—running in place, running up and down stairs, or jogging for good distances outdoors. If you take part in a well-planned running program, you can't help but improve your strength and stamina.

Running helps your lungs to process a greater amount of air with less effort. It strengthens your heart, which also becomes more efficient, pumping more blood with less effort. It increases the number and size of the blood vessels that carry blood to body tissue, another sign of good health.

Running is especially good for those who tend to be overweight, for it helps to convert fat weight to lean weight. You not only feel better when you run—you look better.

How often you run, how far and at what speed depends on many factors, but the advice of a physician and your present level of fitness are the main things to go by. If you haven't been active, begin your program with a series of brisk walks, not runs. Try walking fast for a period of 15 minutes three of four times a week. As your fitness improves, add to what you're doing. Combine running with walking for a period of 20 minutes four times a week. Aim for a level where you're combining jogging and running for a period of 30 minutes four times a week.

Stretching

If you plan to do any serious running or take part in an exercise program, you should always warm up first. Get your muscles limber and your heart and lungs pumping. It only takes five or ten minutes.

The warm-up session should include exercises that stretch the muscles and joints to their fullest extent without straining. Some are simple. Just standing and loosely shaking your hands and arms is a warm-up exercise. So is running in place. (Incidentally, when I'm playing a round of golf, I take longer-than-normal steps on the course. This helps to keep my thigh muscles loose and springy.)

Other exercises involve a number of different muscle systems. You've probably been introduced to some of these

STRETCHING EXERCISE NO. 2

in gym classes.

1. To stretch your lower legs, for example, stand erect, your feet 6 to 12 inches apart. Then simply raise up on your toes, stretching as far as you can. Return to your starting position, then rock back on your heels. Hold that position briefly, then return to start.

2. To stretch the thigh muscles, stand erect, step as far as you can with your left foot, then bend the right knee so it touches the floor. Return to an erect position, then stride forward with the right foot and bend the left knee.

3. The toe touch is another good stretching exercise. Stand erect, your feet about shoulder width apart and your arms extended outward to the sides. Bending at the waist, touch the left toe with the right hand, return to a standing position, then touch left hand to right toe.

4. The squat stretches the muscles of the thighs. Stand erect, your arms out in front of you. Lower your body until

STRETCHING EXERCISE NO. 4

you reach a half-squat position. You'll feel the muscles stretching in the top of your thighs. Hold the position for a few seconds, return to the starting position, then repeat the drill.

5. A one-leg squat stretch is also good. Stand erect with your arms out in front of your body. Put your weight on one foot and extend the other foot forward. Slowly lower yourself to a half-squat position. Your outstretched leg should be parallel to the floor. Repeat the drill three or four times, then switch feet. When you first try this exercise, you may have a problem keeping your balance, but with practice you'll soon overcome that.

6. The hurdler's stretch is a well-known drill. Sit on the floor with the right leg extended and in front of your body, while the left leg, bent at the knee, is out to the side. Reach out with your hands to the side and reach again. Repeat several times. Then reverse the position of your legs and do the drill again, this time reaching toward your left foot.

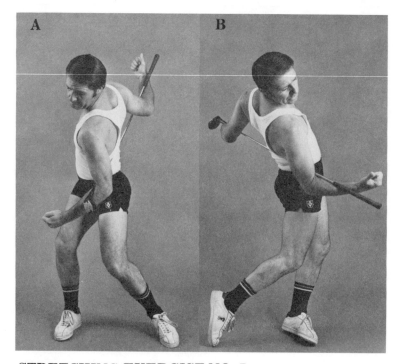

STRETCHING EXERCISE NO. 7

7. To stretch the muscles of my upper back and shoulders, I place a golf club behind my back and hook my arms about the shaft. I then rotate my upper body, first to the right, and then to the left. You can feel the muscles stretching. You can also do this exercise on the golf course, while you're waiting to tee off or anytime you feel tight or tense.

Muscle-Building

There are many exercises you can do to strengthen the muscles important to your golf swing. The most efficient way to build muscles is by weightlifting. Such a program should be planned seriously and directed by a coach or gym teacher. It usually requires barbells and often other equipment. Most of the exercises described below are for those who do not have such gear or do not have access to a gym.

Hands, Wrists, Forearms

1. A simple exercise that you can do to strengthen your forearms, wrists and hands involves the use of a thick bath towel. Fold the towel in quarters, then hold the towel in one hand and twist it with the other hand. Twist it as tightly as you can. Stop, rest, reverse hand positions, and twist again.

2. Or you can get a rubber ball, slightly larger than a golf ball, and one that compresses easily. Grasp the ball and squeeze it tightly. Keep doing it over and over, first with one hand, then with the other. In the days before Arnold Palmer had his own airplane, he used to drive from one tournament to the next. He always kept a small rubber ball in the car, and on long trips he would squeeze the ball with his free hand.

3. I also recommend the use of a hand grip to build finger, wrist and forearm strength. You can buy one in a sporting goods store for about $5. You squeeze the grip by opening and closing your hand. Or you simply hold the

MUSCLE- BUILDER NO. 2

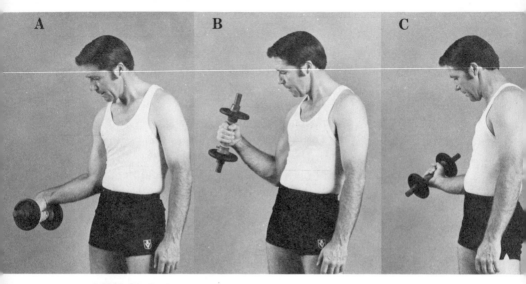

A B C

MUSCLE- BUILDER NO. 4

handles together for as long as you can against the resistance of the springs. You adjust the grip tension by varying the number of springs in use.

Some people say that you can develop your fingers and forearms to such an extent that you can lose your putting touch. I don't agree with this theory. I think you become more sensitive to the feel of the club as you get stronger. You actually improve your touch.

4. A drill that's effective in building the strength of your forearms involves the use of a dumbbell that weighs from five to ten pounds, again depending on your present forearm strength. It's best to start with a five-pound size and work your way up.

Grasp the weight in one hand and put the elbow against your side, keeping your wrist and forearm parallel to the floor. Rotate your hand and wrist, first to the right as far as you can, then to the left. Keep repeating the exercise until your arm begins to tire. Then switch to the other hand.

Beginning from the same starting position, slowly lower the weight to your thigh, then slowly raise it. Turn your hand and arm over and repeat the exercise. Do 10 repetitions with one hand, then switch to the other.

Upper Body Muscles

5. You can also use a dumbbell in a drill that imitates the golf swing. Position your feet about shoulder width apart; bend slightly at the knees. Grasp the dumbbell in your left hand and swing it to your right, turning your upper body, actually imitating the movement of the left arm in the golf swing. Swing the weight at least as high as the level of your head. Once you've reached the top of the backswing, start the weight in the other direction, swinging it down and through. As you take the weight back, be sure to keep your eyes focused on a spot in front of you—focused "on the ball."

6. Another good exercise to develop the upper body muscles involves the use of a steel rod or pipe, about the length of the driver you use and about the weight of a crowbar. A 36-inch length of steel rod, the type used in reinforcing concrete, serves nicely.

Take the rod in both hands, gripping it as if it were a golf club. Keeping your left arm in control, take the "club" all the way back and then swing through. Do it slowly from beginning to end. Keep repeating the exercise until your muscles begin to tire.

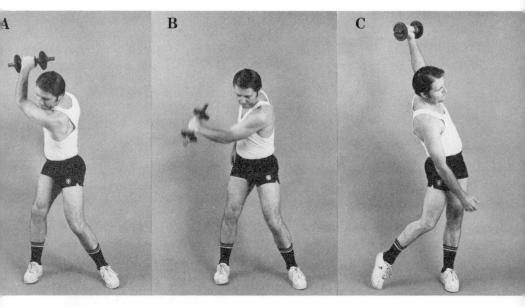

MUSCLE-BUILDER NO. 5

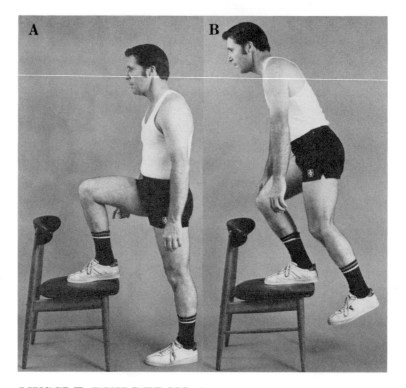

MUSCLE- BUILDER NO. 7

Legs

You need strong legs in golf, because they serve as the foundation of your swing. If your legs begin to tire late in a round, you won't be properly balanced when you swing, and the chances are good that you'll be spending more of your time in the woods looking for lost balls. You need good legs when you putt, too. They give you a steady platform from which to launch your stroke.

7. To build your calf muscles, try an exercise called the chair climb. Get a sturdy chair, one with a seat that is 15 or 16 inches off the floor. Stand facing the chair, then step up onto it with your right foot, stand erect, step down. Then step up with the other foot, the left foot, stand erect, and step down.

8. Another drill I've found of value is what I call the skiing exercise. It's an isometric drill, one in which you

contract your muscles, your thigh muscles in this case, without any body movement. In the skier's exercise, you assume a skier's position—a half-sitting position—with your back pressing against a wall. Press from your back, putting pressure on your legs and feet. Notice how the heavy muscles of your thighs quickly tire. The purpose of the exercise is to strengthen those muscles. Relax; stand erect, then try it again.

As you do the exercises, keep challenging yourself. If you're doing chair climbs and you're doing 12 of them in two minutes, and you keep doing that number at that pace over a long period, you'll eventually be able to do the drill almost effortlessly. Your muscles will become stronger and you'll be able to breeze through the drill.

At this point, make it more challenging by increasing the number of repetitions—in the case of the chair exercises, adding six a week—or stepping up the pace. Instead of doing 12 chair climbs at the rate of six per minute, do eight per minute.

What's said above applies to all of the exercises described in this chapter. Either increase the number of repetitions week by week, or step up the pace.

Your Diet

Exercise represents only one part of a fitness program. You should also plan and follow a sensible diet.

I am very surprised by the number of overweight people I see today. You can't play your best golf if you're overweight.

We are all constantly being tempted by "junk food"— food like hot dogs, hamburgers, pizza and ice cream. These foods, generally speaking, contain what are called "empty calories." They add to your weight but give little in the way of nutrition, so we should all put some limit on how often we eat them.

A sensible daily diet consists mainly of foods from these categories:

Bread and cereal—Four or more servings each day,

with one slice of bread counting as one serving, as does one ounce of dry cereal or ¼ cup of cooked cereal. Eat dark bread instead of white bread.

Fruit and vegetables—At least four servings a day, including a citrus fruit or other source of vitamin C, and a serving of a dark green vegetable at least every other day for vitamin A.

When I travel on the professional tour, I always keep a supply of fresh fruit in my room, and I carry dried fruits with me, too, such as raisins and prunes. I also keep a supply of dried fruits, plus dried seeds and nuts in my golf bag. Should I get hungry during a round, I snack on them.

Meat—Two or more servings per day, with each two or three ounces counting as one serving. I recommend poultry or fish in preference to beef or pork. Sometimes I'll substitute two eggs for a serving of meat.

Milk—Most young golfers should drink two or three glasses of milk a day. Avoid coffee or tea or any other beverage containing stimulants such as caffeine.

My meals are simple. For breakfast I usually have fruit juice, a serving of raisin bran with a sliced banana and milk, two boiled eggs and two slices of whole wheat toast. I also have tea with honey, but the tea is a special brew from which the caffeine has been removed. Three or four hours before a round of golf, I'll have a meal of this type.

I might skip lunch on a golfing day, but I eat fruit during the day. I drink plenty of water throughout the day, including two glasses in the morning and a glass before going to bed. I never put extra salt on my food or take salt tablets. There's enough salt in the food I eat.

My biggest meal is usually the evening meal, when I have a serving of fish or chicken and at least two servings of vegetables, including a baked potato. I'll usually have dessert at the evening meal and decaffeinated coffee.

I pay a lot of attention to how my food is prepared and I go by these three simple rules: 1. Raw fruit and vegetables are better than cooked. 2. Less cooking is better than more. 3. Broiled is better than fried.

Illustrated Glossary of Golf Terms

Ace   Ball hit from the tee into the cup in one stroke; hole-in-one.

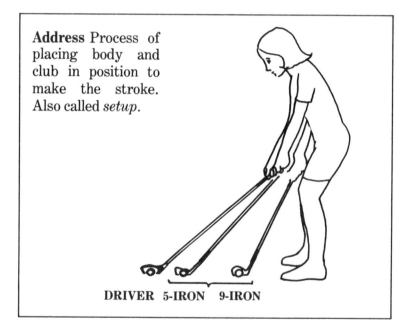

Address Process of placing body and club in position to make the stroke. Also called *setup*.

DRIVER 5-IRON 9-IRON

Amateur   Person who plays golf as a sport, without earning money from it.

Approach   Shot played to green, usually executed with a medium or short iron.

Apron   Area immediately surrounding the green, usually trimmed shorter than the fairway, but not as short as the green. Also called *fringe*.

Away   Ball farthest from the hole, and therefore (according to custom and etiquette) next to be played.

Back door   Side of cup farthest from player.

Back nine   Second nine holes of an 18-hole course.

Backspin   Reverse spin imparted to the ball, causing it to check abruptly upon landing. Also called *bite*.

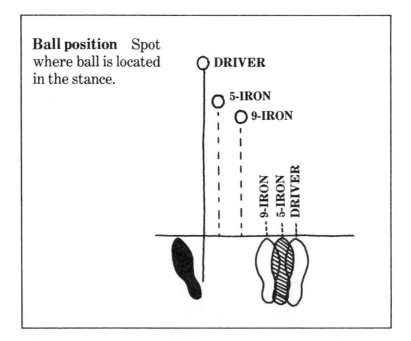

Ball position   Spot where ball is located in the stance.

DRIVER

5-IRON

9-IRON

9-IRON   5-IRON   DRIVER

Banana ball   Shot that curves wildly from left to right (for right-handers); an extreme slice.

Bent   A finely textured type of grass.

Bermuda   A coarsely textured type of grass.

Best ball   Format of play in which the lower score of either of two partners is counted.

Birdie   Score of one stroke less than par for a hole.

Bite   See *backspin*.

Blind hole   Hole where the green is not visible from spot where normal approach shot is played.

Blind shot   Approach shot when golfer cannot see flagstick.

Bogey   Score of one stroke over par for a hole.

Borrow   See *break*.

Brassie   An early name for the 2-wood.

Break   Distance ball will travel to side when putted across slanting green, also called *borrow*.

Bunker   Pit or depression on or along a fairway or next to a green, usually filled with sand. Also called *sand trap*.

Buried lie   Ball imbedded in bunker sand.

Caddie   Someone who carries a golfer's clubs and sometimes gives playing advice.

Carry   Distance a shot travels on the fly.

Casual water   Any temporary accumulation of water (such as a puddle after a rainstorm) not regarded as a water hazard. Rules permit moving ball so you don't have to play through such water.

Chip shot   Short approach shot that flies low. See *pitch*.

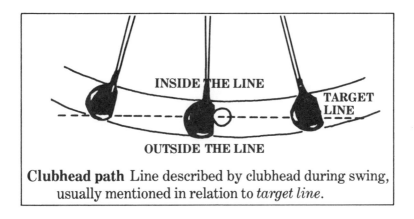

Clubhead path Line described by clubhead during swing, usually mentioned in relation to *target line*.

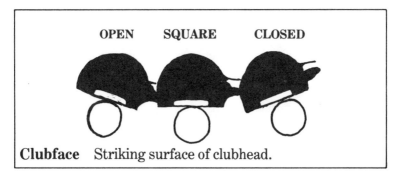

Clubface Striking surface of clubhead.

Collar Grass growing around edges of green (fringe) or bunker.

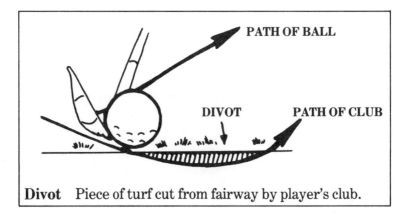

Divot Piece of turf cut from fairway by player's club.

Dogleg Hole with a fairway that bends right or left.

Dormie   Situation in match play, in which a player or team are ahead by the same number of holes as remain to be played.

Double bogey   Score of two strokes over par for a hole.

Double eagle   Score of three strokes under par for a hole.

Draw   Shot with a slight curve from right to left (for right-handers).

Driver   The No. 1 wood, longest and least lofted.

Dub   To hit the ball poorly; also a poor golfer.

Duck Hook   Shot which curves sharply to left and also nosedives.

Duffer   Poor golfer.

Eagle   Score of two strokes under par for a hole.

Explosion shot   Shot from a bunker in which a large amount of sand is displaced by clubhead, forcing ball up and out.

Fade   Shot with a slight curve from left to right (for right-handers).

Fairway   Mowed area of the course between tee and green.

Fat shot   Shot in which club hits ground before hitting ball, reducing distance; also called chili dip.

Flag or flagstick   On a green the pole marking exact location of the cup. Also called pin.

Flier lie   Ball resting in high grass, causing shot to fly without control of backspin.

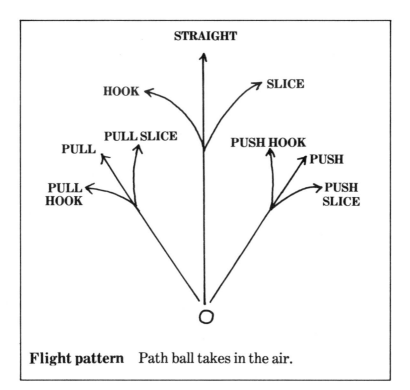

Flight pattern   Path ball takes in the air.

"Fore!"   Warning cry to persons in danger of being hit by a shot.

Forward press   Slight movement of some part of body, usually the hands or knees, toward target prior to start of swing.

Foursome   Group of four golfers playing together; also a form of competition in which two partners play against another team, with each pair playing one ball.

Fringe   See *apron*.

Front nine   First nine holes of an 18-hole course.

Gimme putt   Very short putt, usually within 12–18 inches, that an opponent in a match frequently will concede.

Golf course The entire area over which play is permitted.
(Arrows show best way to play each hole.)

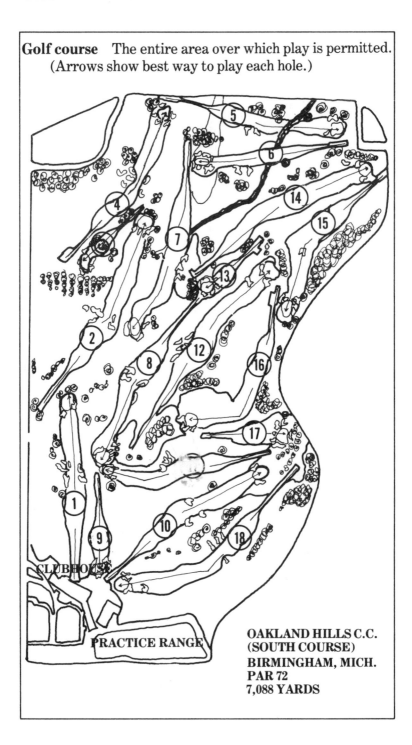

OAKLAND HILLS C.C.
(SOUTH COURSE)
BIRMINGHAM, MICH.
PAR 72
7,088 YARDS

Grain   Direction in which certain types of flat-lying grass grow on a green.

Green   Putting surface of closely mown grass where each hole ends.

Gross score   Total number of strokes on a hole or course before handicap is deducted.

Hacker   Poor golfer.

Handicap   Numerical rating of a player's ability in relation to shooting par, based on most recent previous 18-hole scores, allowing golfer to compete on even terms with individuals of varying ability.

Hanging lie   Ball in an extreme downhill lie.

Halved   In match play, hole is said to be halved when each player on side plays it in same score.

Hazard   Any bunker or body of water on the course.

High side   Area above cup on sloping green.

Hole high   Approach shot that stops to the right or left of the hole and about even with it; also called pin high.

Hole out   Putting the ball into the cup to finish play on a hole.

Honor   Privilege of being the first player to drive from the tee; accorded to the player winning the preceding hole.

Hook   Shot that veers sharply from right to left (or from left to right for lefties). See *flight pattern*.

Imbedded lie   Ball buried in soft turf.

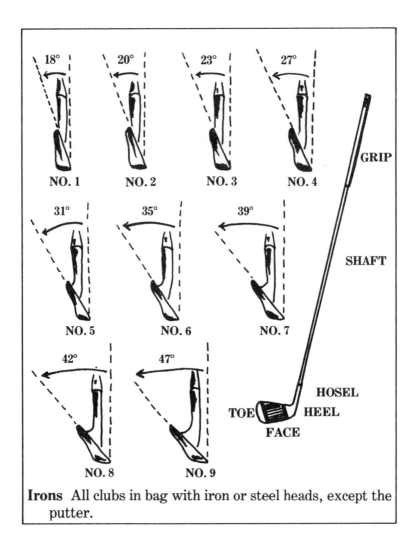

18° NO. 1 20° NO. 2 23° NO. 3 27° NO. 4
31° NO. 5 35° NO. 6 39° NO. 7
42° NO. 8 47° NO. 9

GRIP
SHAFT
HOSEL
TOE HEEL
FACE

Irons All clubs in bag with iron or steel heads, except the putter.

Lag On green, to aim a long putt to finish near hole rather than to hole out.

Lie Spot where ball rests after a stroke; *also*, the angle at which the shaft is fitted to the clubhead.

Links A golf course along seacoast, laid out on sandy soil left by receding ocean tides.

Lip Rim of the cup.

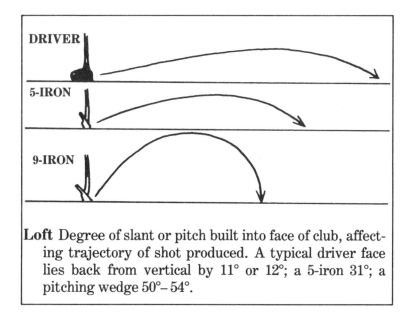

Loft Degree of slant or pitch built into face of club, affecting trajectory of shot produced. A typical driver face lies back from vertical by 11° or 12°; a 5-iron 31°; a pitching wedge 50°– 54°.

Low side Area below cup on sloping green.

Mashie An early name for an iron, equal to today's 5- or 6-iron.

Match play Competition between two players or teams in which the winner is determined by the number of holes won, rather than number of strokes.

Medal play See *stroke play.*

Mulligan Second chance to hit a tee shot, usually on the first hole, when the first try has ended poorly. Common in informal play but illegal under the Rules.

Nassau Form of competition in which one point is scored for winning the first nine holes, one point for winning the second nine, and one point for winning the entire 18 holes.

Net score Player's score after handicap strokes have been deducted.

Niblick   Early name for a club with about the loft of the modern 9-iron.

Obstruction   Anything artificial, whether erected, placed or left on the course, which interferes with play. The ball may be moved away from an obstruction without penalty, or the obstruction itself may be moved, again with no penalty.

Out-of-bounds (OB)   Area of the course where play is prohibited. When a player hits a ball out-of-bounds, he must replay the stroke from a spot as near as possible to where the original shot was made, and take a one-stroke penalty.

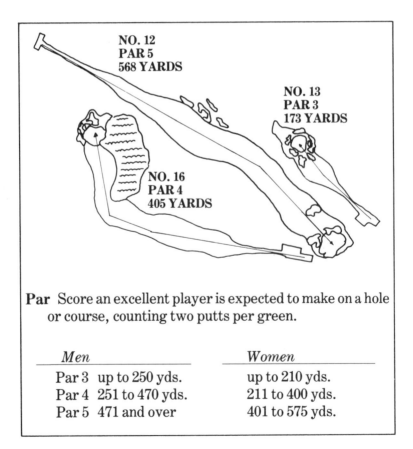

NO. 12
PAR 5
568 YARDS

NO. 13
PAR 3
173 YARDS

NO. 16
PAR 4
405 YARDS

Par   Score an excellent player is expected to make on a hole or course, counting two putts per green.

Men	*Women*
Par 3 up to 250 yds.	up to 210 yds.
Par 4 251 to 470 yds.	211 to 400 yds.
Par 5 471 and over	401 to 575 yds.

Penalty stroke A stroke added to a player's score for a violation of the rules.

Pin See *flagstick*.

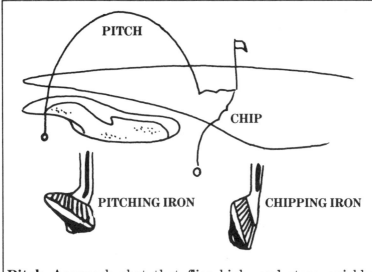

Pitch Approach shot that flies high, and stops quickly upon landing, made with a highly-lofted club.

Professional Person who earns money playing golf, as teacher or competitor.

Provisional ball Extra ball played when a previous shot is believed lost or out-of-bounds.

Pull Shot that travels straight, but to the left of target. See *flight pattern* .

Punch shot Shot played with reduced stroke and with hands well forward at address, producing lower-than-normal trajectory.

Push Shot that travels straight, but to the right of target. See *flight pattern*.

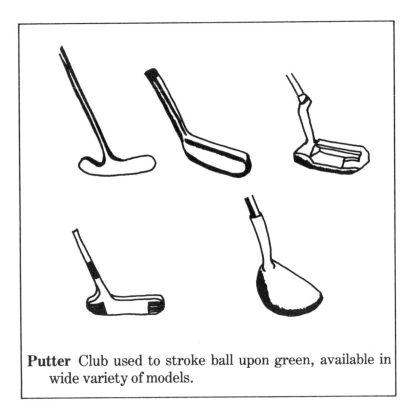

Putter Club used to stroke ball upon green, available in wide variety of models.

Putt Stroke made on the green.

Recovery shot Shot played from the rough, sand or other trouble area toward the green.

Rim Describes a putt that rolls around the edge of cup but stays out.

Rough Area of untended terrain bordering fairways, consisting usually of long grass, weeds, shrubs, etc.

Round Complete circuit of 18 holes.

Rub of the Green A shot stopped or deflected by an outside agency.

Sand trap See *bunker*.

PEBBLE BEACH GOLF LINKS

Out of bounds designated by white marked stakes. U.S.G.A. Rules govern all play except where local rules prevail. The ocean shall be played as a lateral hazard. Please replace divots, repair ball marks on the greens and rake sand traps.

HOLES	YARDS CHAMPIONSHIP TEES	YARDS REGULAR TEES	PAR	LADIES' TEES	HANDICAP STROKES						
1	385	375	4	320	8						
2	507	432	5	360	10						
3	368	320	4	265	12						
4	325	300	4	250	16						
5	180	160	3	140	14						
6	515	470	5	395	2						
7	120	110	3	100	18						
8	425	400	4	360	6						
9	450	425	4	320	4						
TOTAL OUT	3275	2992	36	2510							
10	436	406	4	326	7						
11	380	380	4	325	5						
12	205	185	3	170	17						
13	400	380	4	292	9						
14	555	545	5	430	1						
15	406	365	4	305	13						
16	400	375	4	310	11						
17	218	185	3	180	15						
18	540	530	5	425	3						
TOTAL IN	3540	3351	36	2763							
TOTAL OUT	3275	2992	36	2510							
TOTAL	6815	6343	72	5273							
SELF											
OPPONENT				DATE							

Scorecard Card showing par and yardage for each hole and used to record stroke and match play.

Scratch player Golfer with a handicap of zero.

Setup See *address*.

Shank   To hit the ball with neck or hosel of the club, usually sending it sharply to the right.

Skull   See *top*.

Sky   To hit a shot extremely high and to a much shorter distance than intended.

Slice   Shot which curves sharply from left to right (or from right to left for lefties). See *flight pattern* .

Sole   Bottom of clubhead; *also*, to place club on the ground at address.

Spoon   An early term to describe a wood with about the loft of a modern 3-wood.

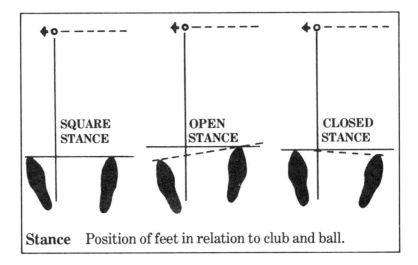

SQUARE STANCE   OPEN STANCE   CLOSED STANCE

Stance   Position of feet in relation to club and ball.

Stroke play   Competition in which the winner is decided by the total number of strokes taken for an entire round or series of rounds; also called *medal play*.

Summer rules   Playing under the official rules with no provision for a player improving lie of ball except under special conditions.

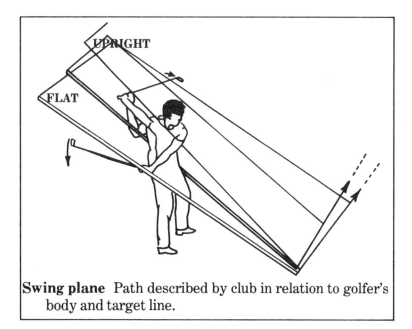

Swing plane Path described by club in relation to golfer's body and target line.

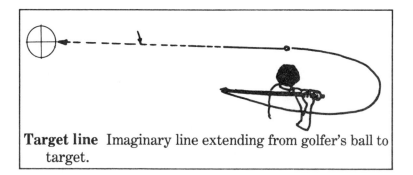

Target line Imaginary line extending from golfer's ball to target.

Tee Wooden or plastic peg upon which the ball is placed for the drive; *also*, the area from which the ball is driven at the beginning of play on a hole.

Tee off To drive a ball off a tee.

Texas wedge Putter when used off the green.

Thin shot Shot in which club strikes ball too high up, producing lower-than-normal flight.

Through the green   All the area on any given hole except for the teeing ground, green and hazards.

Toe   To hit a shot on or near the toe of club.

Top   To mis-hit shot by striking ball above its center with bottom edge of club.

Trap   See *bunker*.

Unplayable lie   Ball finishing in spot from which golfer judges it is impossible to advance to next shot. Under the Rules, player may move ball to playable spot, taking one-stroke penalty.

Up   Number of holes or strokes a player is ahead of opponent.

Waggle   A slight preliminary movement made prior to the backswing as an aid to relaxation and tempo.

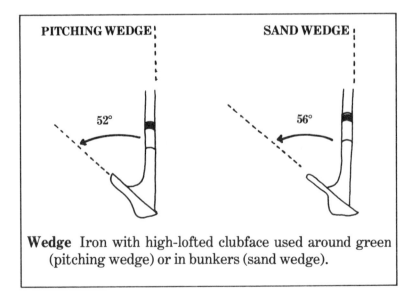

Wedge Iron with high-lofted clubface used around green (pitching wedge) or in bunkers (sand wedge).

Whiff   To miss the ball completely.

Winter Rules Local practice of allowing players to move ball to better spots on fairway when conditions are poor; not recognized under the official Rules of Golf.

Woods Long-shafted clubs with wooden or composite heads, used for long shots off tee and fairway.

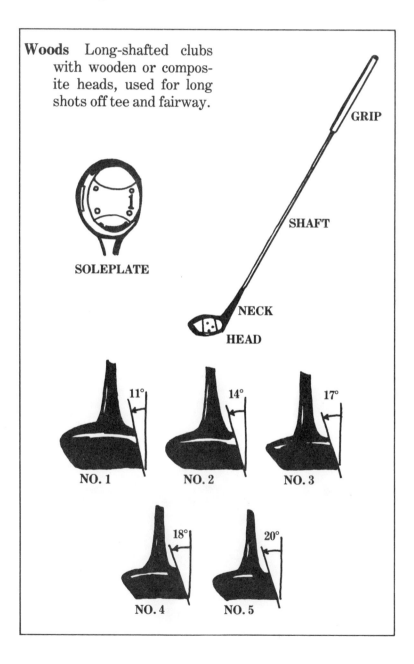

GRIP

SHAFT

SOLEPLATE

NECK

HEAD

11° NO. 1

14° NO. 2

17° NO. 3

18° NO. 4

20° NO. 5

A NOTE ON THE
PRODUCTION OF THIS BOOK

This book was typeset by IceType,
Westport, Connecticut; printed
and bound by Book Press,
Brattleboro, Vermont.
     The paper is Clear Spring
Offset, manufactured by
Westvaco Paper Company.